# Africans Thought of It

# Africans Thought of It

## AMAZING INNOVATIONS

**Bathseba Opini**

**Richard B. Lee**

annick press
toronto + new york + vancouver

Cover and interior design by Sheryl Shapiro
Edited by David MacDonald
Maps on pages 10–11 and illustrations on page 19 by Martha Newbigging

A sincere thank-you to expert reader Dr. Silvia Forni, Associate Curator, Royal Ontario Museum.

Annick Press Ltd.


We acknowledge the support of the Canada Council for the Arts, the Ontario Arts Council, and the Government of Canada through the Canada Book Fund (CBF) for our publishing activities.

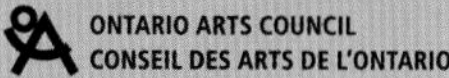


**Cataloging in Publication**

Opini, Bathseba
Africans thought of it : amazing innovations / Bathseba Opini, Richard B. Lee.

(We thought of it)
Includes bibliographical references and index.
ISBN 978-1-55451-277-5 (bound).—ISBN 978-1-55451-276-8 (pbk.)

1. Africa—Civilization—Juvenile literature. 2. Africa—Intellectual life—Juvenile literature. 3. Inventions—Africa—Juvenile literature. I. Lee, Richard, 1937- II. Title. III. Series: We thought of it

DT4.O65 2011 j960 C2010-907063-1

Distributed in Canada by:
Firefly Books Ltd.
66 Leek Crescent
Richmond Hill, ON
L4B 1H1

Published in the U.S.A. by:
Annick Press (U.S.) Ltd.
Distributed in the U.S.A. by:
Firefly Books (U.S.) Inc.
P.O. Box 1338
Ellicott Station
Buffalo, NY 14205

Watch for more books in the *We Thought of It* series, coming soon.

Printed in China.

**Visit us at: www.annickpress.com**

**For all my family members and friends, and for the children of Africa—with love and admiration.**
**—B.O.**

**To my African friends and colleagues Scholastica, Pombili, Gakekoshe, and their children; to my children David, Miriam, Lucah, and in memory of Alex.**
**—R.L.**

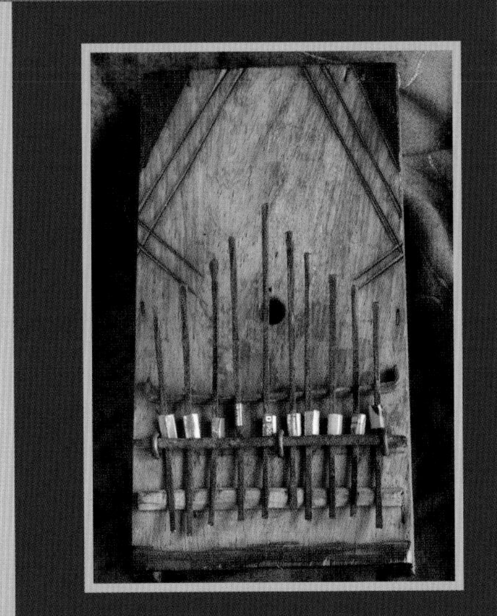

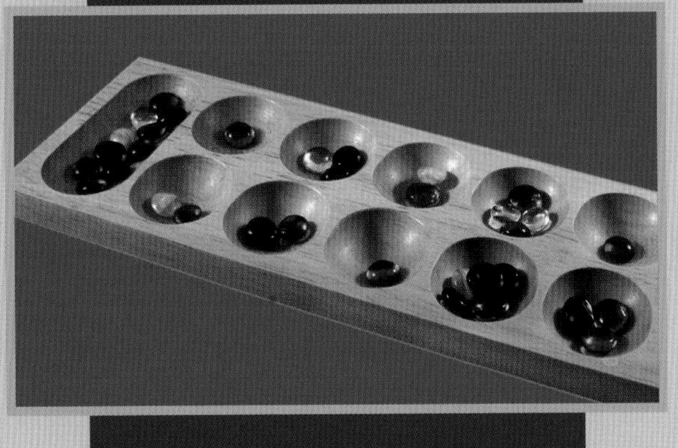

# Contents

# Karibu, Soo Dhawow, Kamogelo

Bathseba picks tea on her father's farm in Kenya.

A tea plantation in Kenya

My name is Bathseba and I grew up near Keroka, a small town in western Kenya. My family belongs to a cultural group called the Abagusii. As a young girl, I spent lots of time with my parents, grandparents, uncles, and aunts, who taught me about the Abagusii customs by sharing traditional tales, riddles, proverbs, and other wise sayings.

When I wasn't in school, I helped out with chores on the farm. For example, I helped my mom plant, weed, and harvest millet. She taught me traditional ways of scaring away the birds that came to eat our crops.

I also helped out my dad, who grew tea. I would go with my siblings early in the morning to pick tea. Sometimes we also herded cows, sheep, and goats. This was lots of fun because we would also sing songs and play games while we were out in the field herding animals.

Now that I live in Canada, there are many things I miss from my life in Africa: the beautiful natural landscapes, the night sky filled with bright stars, the way the moon seemed to smile down at me,

# Welcome.

and the wonderful hospitality of African people. But most of all I miss my family and friends, and hearing the stories and proverbs that are part of my cultural heritage. My love for Africa is part of me, and I carry it with me wherever I go. I hope this book will help you understand why I love the people and places of Africa so much.

Johannesburg is the largest city in South Africa.

Africa is the world's second-largest continent and home to almost 1 billion people. Over 800 different ethnic groups live in the 54 countries on the continent. While many Africans live in peaceful rural villages and practice traditional forms of agriculture, Africa has some of the world's largest and busiest cities, such as Cairo (Egypt), Lagos (Nigeria), Johannesburg (South Africa), and Khartoum (Sudan).

Ancient ruins in Zimbabwe

Africa's history includes the very beginning of human history. The earliest ancestors of modern humans lived in Africa over 4 million years ago. Farming and herding developed thousands of years ago and, over time, great empires arose in west, central, and southern Africa. Countries such as Ghana, Mali, and Zimbabwe take their names from powerful ancient kingdoms.

Mount Kilimanjaro in Tanzania is the highest mountain in Africa.

Dried calabash gourds are used for storing liquids, just as we use bottles.

Today, many aspects of African culture have spread around the globe. For example, plants used in traditional African medicine are now used to make modern medicines and cosmetics. Museums in North America and Europe have large collections of traditional African art. Much of the music that is popular today has been influenced by the sounds and rhythms of African music.

My co-author Richard Lee and I invite you to join us on a fascinating journey to discover some of the amazing innovations of African peoples.

A traditional wooden pillow from Ethiopia

The Gaborone International Convention Centre, Botswana

## A Note from Richard Lee

My research in Africa began in 1963, in the village of Dobe in Botswana. At that time, the San people of Dobe still lived a traditional lifestyle, which was very unusual even back then. Women gathered wild nuts, berries, and roots. Men hunted with bows and arrows. I had chosen Dobe because it was a place where the traditional hunting and gathering way of life could still be observed.

One night, I heard a strange melodic sound coming from a neighboring village and went to investigate. The light of a fire revealed a circle of singing women. Men were dancing rhythmically around them. Soon one man staggered and fell into a deep trance. He stood up and moved from person to person, laying his hands on each one—including me. I was witnessing the famous and ancient San medicine dance.

That trip convinced me that Africa was where I wanted to center my life's work and I have returned many times since then. Life has changed in Dobe, and young people now sit at their computers and surf the internet.

I have been deeply impressed by the African innovations I have seen, many of which are featured in this book. From hunters using leaf beetle larvae to obtain poison for arrows, to people crafting uniquely African tools from metal—the peoples of Africa have demonstrated their outstanding skill at creating useful innovations. This tradition continues today, with many Africans applying their gift for innovation to the challenges of a high-tech world.

I am delighted to be able to share with readers some of the wonders of African innovation.

Richard enjoys a laugh with a friend in Africa.

# MAPS OF AFRICA TODAY

Mediterranean Sea
Atlas Mountains
Sahara Desert
Nile River
Niger River
Nile River
Congo River
Lake Victoria
Atlantic Ocean
Mount Kilimanjaro
Kalahari
Desert
Indian Ocean

# HUNTING

Thousands of years before guns and motor vehicles were invented, African hunters developed skills to help them hunt. There are still some hunters who use the same skills today.

## Tracking Techniques

African hunters became very skilled at using animal tracks to help them hunt. For example, young hunters of the San people (sometimes called Bushmen) of Botswana and Namibia learned the following skills from their fathers:

- Hunters learned to recognize the tracks left by many different kinds of animals. They could also tell whether the tracks had been left by a male or female animal, and whether the animal was young or fully grown. From the tracks, hunters could also learn whether the animal was traveling alone or in a herd.
- By carefully examining the tracks, hunters could tell how long ago the animal had been there. If the tracks had been made a few minutes or hours before, there was a good chance the hunters could catch up with the animal. If the tracks had been made a day or two before, the animal was probably too far away.
- From the tracks, hunters could tell how quickly the animal was traveling. It might have stopped to eat or rest in the shade, or it might not have stopped at all. This information helped hunters to guess how close or far the animal might be.
- The tracks might also tell hunters if an animal was sick or injured. An animal that is not able to move quickly is easier to hunt.

Over thousands of years, these skills have helped hunters and their families survive in conditions that were often difficult.

**A Maasai man takes a digital photo of fresh lion tracks.**

## The First Scientists?

When the famous astronomer Carl Sagan learned about the tracking techniques used by ancient San hunters, he said they must have been the first scientists. Why would he think so? Like scientists, the hunters looked carefully at evidence (the animal tracks), and tried to understand what it meant.

In the modern sport of archery, people practice their skill using a bow and arrow.

## Bow and Arrow

Some experts believe that the bow and arrow is an African invention. The earliest evidence is arrow points made from bone, which were discovered in a cave in South Africa. These arrow points are about 60,000 years old.

Early bows were made from wood, and the bowstring was made from animal sinew, animal skin, or plant material. Stone and bone were used to make arrows, but in later times iron was used.

By about 5000 years ago, the bow and arrow had become an important weapon for ancient Egyptians, who used it in battle as well as for hunting.

Ancient Ethiopians were famous for their skill with the bow and arrow. The bows they used were about 2 meters (6 feet) long.

Arrowheads were made in a variety of shapes.

## Deadly Poisons

Putting poison on an arrow made the bow and arrow a more effective weapon for hunting.

Traditional African hunters often used plants to make poison. In some places, hunters used a plant called kombé (pronounced *kom-bay*). They crushed the plant's leaves and seeds to make a thick paste that they rubbed on arrows. Arrows poisoned with kombé killed animals almost instantly.

The San people discovered that it was possible to get poison for arrows from the larvae or chrysalids of leaf beetles. (The larvae are young, wingless beetles that look like caterpillars.) This poison did not kill as quickly as kombé, but it was still effective. An arrow with leaf beetle poison could kill an antelope weighing 200 kilograms (440 pounds) in 24 hours. Hunters would follow the animal until it was no longer able to move.

A San hunter applies poison from a beetle chrysalis to an arrow.

# AGRICULTURE

How did early African peoples get food? They hunted animals, gathered foods such as nuts and berries, and fished. With the discovery of agriculture, African peoples began to grow crops and raise animals much like modern farmers do.

## Planting Millet

Millet is a plant that produces small seeds that people use as food. It was an important crop for ancient African farmers, but there was a problem with planting the seeds. If farmers plowed the field before scattering the seeds, the seeds were clearly visible on the dark earth and would be eaten by birds and other animals.

African farmers came up with some solutions to this problem. Grasses and other plants would have been growing in the field before it was plowed. Farmers discovered that they could scatter the seeds on a field before plowing it, and the plants already growing would hide the seeds from animals. Once the seeds sprouted, the field could be plowed and the sprouts would continue to grow. Sometimes farmers didn't plow the field and left the millet to grow among the grasses and other plants.

Another solution was to scatter the seeds on plowed land, and then use a branch to work the seeds down into the soil. That way, they would be hidden from animals.

**Workers in Benin thresh millet to separate the seeds from the plant.**

## Watermelon

Watermelon grows wild in Africa, and people in southern and central Africa were the first to grow watermelons as crops. As the name suggests, watermelons contain lots of water, so they were an important source of water for people in times of drought.

The planting of watermelon spread to other areas of Africa over time. Experts believe that the ancient Egyptians began growing watermelon more than 5000 years ago.

**Watermelons growing wild in the Sahara Desert**

## Oil Palm

There are many different kinds of palm trees. The African oil palm, which first grew in western Africa, has been an important food source for some Africans since as far back as ancient times. Experts have found evidence that palm oil was used in Egypt about 5000 years ago.

The fruit of the oil palm grows in bunches, which can weigh 10 kilograms (22 pounds) or more. From the fruit early Africans obtained palm oil, which is very nutritious and was used for cooking. Palm oil was also used as a medicine for treating bruises and sprains.

To get palm oil from the fruit, people boiled the fruit for several hours to soften it. Then they used a wooden mortar and pestle to pound the fruit into a soft, wet pulp. Sometimes, people just walked on the boiled fruit to create pulp. Then palm oil was squeezed out of the pulp.

Just as maple trees are tapped to get sap for making maple syrup, palm trees were tapped to get a sweet juice that was used to make palm wine.

In the mid-1800s CE, farmers in western Africa began to grow the oil palm as a crop, and palm oil was sold to countries outside Africa. Today, oil palm is a very important crop in Africa. Palm oil is used in many different products, including margarine, chocolate, soaps, detergent, candles, and cosmetics.

## Coffee

Most experts believe that coffee first grew in Africa. It was discovered growing wild in Ethiopia around 600 CE and still grows wild there today. From Africa, the popularity of coffee spread to Arabia and eventually to other continents. Today, coffee is one of the most popular drinks in the world.

Some of the coffee people in North America drink is made from coffee beans grown on African farms. Twenty-five African countries grow coffee to sell around the world, but Uganda, Ivory Coast, and Ethiopia are the main exporters of coffee beans.

**A coffee farmer in Uganda removes the husk from the outside of coffee beans.**

*For more information on African food, see pages 32–33.*
*For information on metal tools used by farmers, see pages 20–21.*

# ARCHITECTURE

Throughout history, African peoples have demonstrated their skill in architecture—from the huge pyramids of ancient Egypt to the temporary homes built by the Maasai people of eastern Africa.

## Great Zimbabwe

In the country of Zimbabwe in the south of Africa, there are ruins of magnificent stone structures that together are known as Great Zimbabwe. The construction of this complex of walls and buildings began sometime in the 11th century CE and continued for over 300 years. As many as 18,000 people once lived in these structures.

The walls in Great Zimbabwe are up to 6 meters (20 feet) thick and 12 meters (39 feet) high. One interesting feature is a tower built in the shape of a cone.

Great Zimbabwe was once the center of an empire. The modern country Zimbabwe is named after the ruins.

**Some of the massive stone walls of Great Zimbabwe are still standing today.**

**Above: A close view of a wall of the University of Timbuktu**
**Below: The University of Timbuktu**

## Wattle and Daub

Wattle and daub is a building technique that has been used for about 6000 years. Branches or strips of wood are woven tightly together around a structure of upright poles to form the wattle, which is like a skeleton for a wall. Then a wet mixture called daub is created using ingredients such as clay, mud, straw, animal dung, and water. The wattle is covered with daub and left to dry.

In the ancient kingdoms of western Africa, people used wattle and daub to construct buildings that were much taller than houses made using this method. For example, at the University of Timbuktu in Mali, wattle and daub was used to create buildings with five or six floors. These buildings provided living space for people who came to study at this famous university during medieval times.

## Pyramids of Egypt

The pyramids of Egypt are some of the greatest architectural achievements of humankind. They were built as tombs for the pharaohs, the rulers of ancient Egypt.

The Great Pyramid of Giza (also called the Pyramid of Khufu or the Pyramid of Cheops) took many thousands of workers about 20 years to build. It was finally completed around 2551 BCE. For over 3800 years, the Great Pyramid was the tallest structure in the world.

The pyramid was built from huge blocks of stone, some of which weigh 80 tonnes (88 tons). Workers carefully carved the blocks so they would fit together exactly.

It is amazing that Egyptians were able to build the pyramids using ancient technology. Experts still don't know for sure how they did it.

## Inkajijik

The Maasai people of Kenya and Tanzania built a traditional style of house called an inkajijik. Because the Maasai moved from place to place as they herded their animals, their houses were not built to last a long time.

Women built these houses using mud, sticks, grass, and cow dung. An inkajijik could be circular or star-shaped, and the walls were only about 1.5 meters (5 feet) tall. The houses were built close together to form a village (called a *manyatta*), which was surrounded by a wall constructed by young Maasai warriors.

The Maasai still build this style of house today.

## Rondavel

The rondavel is a round house that has been popular in Africa for centuries. The curved wall was built using the wattle and daub technique. When the wall was dry, it was painted with whitewash and sometimes decorated with beautiful geometric designs.

The roof was made using wattle without daub. When it was ready, ten or more people worked together to place it on top of the house. Then the roof was covered with bundles of dried grass that were tied down to keep them in place. A skillfully made roof would not leak, even in heavy rain.

Rondavels are still built today, although they may have walls made of blocks or bricks and a tin roof.

Above: A rondavel in South Africa; (right) a rondavel in Burkina Faso

# WORKING WITH METAL

For a long time, experts believed that African peoples learned how to work with metal from people who came from outside Africa. But evidence has shown that African peoples developed this skill on their own, possibly as early as 2000 or 3000 BCE. The technology for working with metal made it possible to create a variety of metal tools, weapons, and other objects.

## Smelting

Metals are found in ore (a mixture of metal and rock). Smelting is the process used to separate the metal from the rock. The ore is heated to a very high temperature, which makes the metal melt. Then the metal is collected so it can be made into useful objects.

Ore containing iron has to be heated to about 1400 degrees Celsius (2500 degrees Fahrenheit) in order for the iron to melt. To create such a high temperature, Africans built special furnaces.

Ore

A modern ironworker in Botswana creates an iron tool.

An old smelting furnace in the Democratic Republic of the Congo

## Furnaces

African communities used various types of furnaces for smelting. The traditional furnace shown below was used by the Dimi people of Ethiopia. The walls were made from clay mixed with other materials, such as animal dung and straw, to make the walls stronger.

1) The furnace was packed with dry grass, which was set on fire. Then charcoal was added.
2) Once the charcoal was red hot, clay pipes were inserted into the sides of the furnace. Then clay bowls were attached to the pipes and the tops of the bowls were covered with goatskin.
3) Layers of charcoal and ore were poured into the chimney.
4) People used the clay bowls as bellows. They pushed down on the goatskin over and over again to force the air in the bowl into the furnace. This made the fire hotter.
5) When the iron had melted and separated from the ore, the furnace was left to cool overnight. Then a person climbed down the chimney to collect the iron, which could be made into various objects.

**The furnace is packed with dry grass, which will be set on fire (step 1).**

**Layers of charcoal and ore are poured into the chimney (step 3).**

**Air from the bellows makes the fire grow hotter (step 4).**

## Benin Bronzes

Nigeria's Benin City, which was once a kingdom, was famous for its metal sculptures. These sculptures are often called "Benin bronzes" even though they are made of brass.

Artists began making Benin bronzes around 1400 CE. Early sculptures often showed the king, or "Oba," of Benin, and sometimes animals such as leopards. Along with sculptures, artists also made decorative plaques that often showed members of the king's family and scenes of life in the royal palace.

**This Benin bronze, which shows the head of a king, was made between 1600 CE and 1750 CE.**

# WORKING WITH METAL *continued*

## Money

Ancient African cultures did not have money similar to what we use today. Instead, various cultures used things such as bracelets, blades, or special pieces of cloth the same way we use coins and paper bills. The photos below show some metal objects that were used as money in various parts of Africa.

**A bracelet from Nigeria**

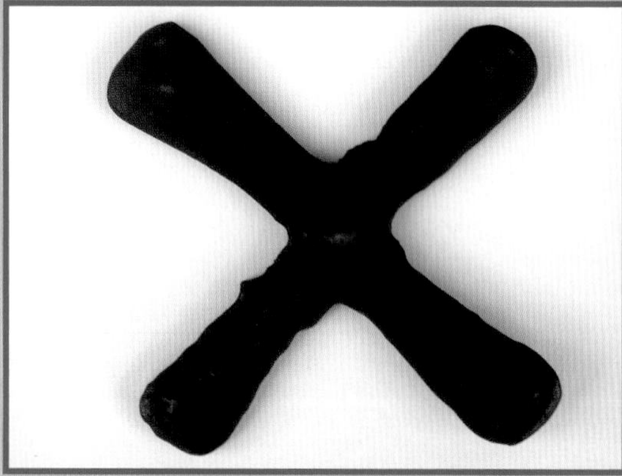

**Cross-shaped money from the Democratic Republic of the Congo**

**Leaf-shaped money from Benin**

## Maresha

The development of the plow allowed farmers to work land much more efficiently than by using a hoe, such as the hilaire (see below). One traditional African plow used in Ethiopia was called a maresha. It had a metal point connected to a wooden arm. On each side of the metal point there were pieces of wood that pushed the soil aside. A long pole connected the plowing tool to a yoke, which allowed two oxen to pull the plow. The farmer held on to the wooden arm while plowing. He could adjust the angle of the arm to control how deeply the metal point cut into the soil.

## Hilaire

The hilaire is a traditional type of hoe that has been used for centuries in western Africa. This type of hoe is very effective for controlling weeds. The metal blade is pushed down into the soil about 5 centimeters (2 inches) below the surface. As the hilaire is moved back and forth, the blade cuts the roots of weeds.

Above: A traditional ax, probably from eastern Africa

Right: This round knife was made by the Turkana people of Kenya. It was worn around the wrist and used in combat.

Below: These shaving blades from the Congo region were also used for trimming fingernails.

A young man from Tanzania carries an iklwa.

## Iklwa

According to legend, it was the Zulu emperor Shaka who invented the iklwa, or Zulu stabbing spear. Other types of spears were quite long and were thrown at enemies, which left the warrior without a weapon. The iklwa is a short spear, about 1 meter (3 feet) long, with a wide metal blade from 36 to 46 centimeters (14 to 18 inches) long. It was used to stab enemies during close combat. The warrior did not let go of the iklwa, so he did not lose his weapon.

## Hunga Munga

The hunga munga is a deadly weapon that could be used like a dagger in hand-to-hand combat. It could also be thrown to make it spin as it flew through the air toward an enemy. When not used in battle, the hunga munga also served as a tool for farming and building.

This weapon was used in many parts of Africa, and was also known by different names in different places. Some of these names include *danisco*, *goleyo*, and *njiga*.

# MEDICINE AND HEALING

Long before the discoveries of modern medicine, traditional African communities had healers who were able to diagnose illnesses. These healers were experts in treating illnesses with various plants that grew wild in the African landscape.

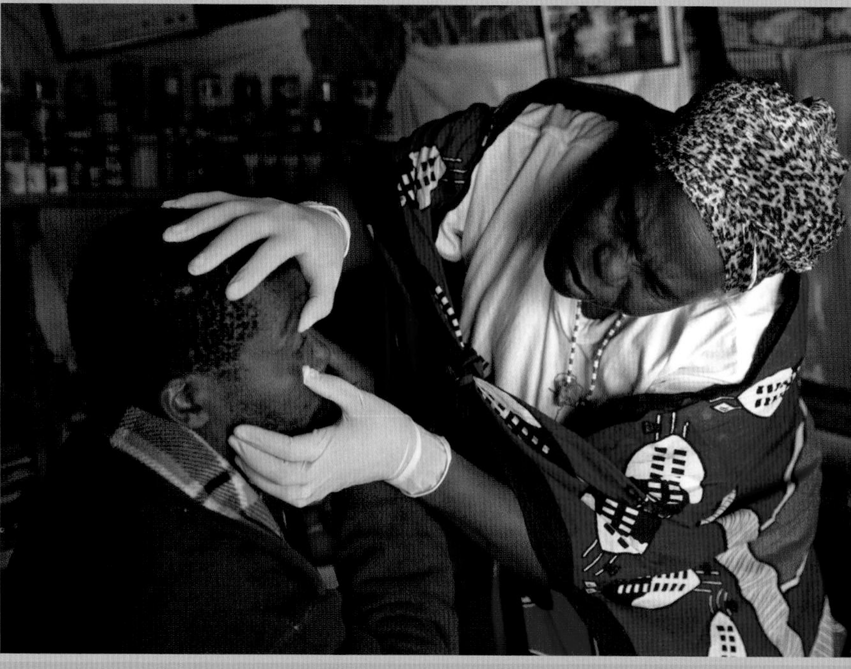

A traditional healer in South Africa

## Becoming a Healer

Diagnosing illnesses and treating them with medicines made from plants was a skill that was passed down from generation to generation. Young people sometimes learned this skill from a parent, but often they received training from a healer in the community.

Training to become a healer took a long time. Among other things, future healers learned

- how to identify the plants used to make medicines, and where to find them
- which parts of a plant to collect (bark, leaves, roots, stems, or flowers)
- how to grind up the plant parts and combine them to make various medicines
- how much medicine to use when treating different illnesses

Healers kept their special knowledge secret and passed it on only to people who were training to become healers.

## Medicines from Plants

There are many plants that were traditionally used as medicines in Africa. Here are just a few, with some examples of how they were used.

| Plant | Used as a Treatment For... |
|---|---|
| South African geranium (roots) | Coughs, colds, bronchitis, breathing problems |
| Balloon pea (all parts) | Poor appetite, upset stomach, cough, asthma, fevers |
| African ginger (roots) | Headache, colds, cough, flu |
| Balsam pear (leaves and fruit) | Upset stomach, burns, chapped skin, frostbite, headache |
| Kinkeliba (roots, bark, leaves) | Wounds, fever, colds, flu, aches, swollen feet |

Balsam pear

Aloe vera

## Aloe Vera

Aloe vera first grew in the warm, dry climate of Africa. Leaves from the aloe vera plant were ground into a powder that was used as medicine to treat wounds (such as from poison arrows or snakebites), burns, and other skin conditions. Hunters used this plant to reduce perspiration so that animals would not notice the scent of a human nearby.

Today, aloe vera is still used to treat wounds and burns. It is also used in many skin products, such as lotions and sunscreens. Scientists are investigating whether aloe vera is effective for treating cancer and other diseases.

## Baobab Tree

Baobab trees grow all over Africa and some experts believe that they can live for thousands of years. African peoples call the baobab the "tree of life" because it provides shelter from the sun, and its leaves, seeds, and fruit are nutritious foods.

Since ancient times, the leaves, fruit, and bark of the baobab have been used to make medicines. Traditional healers used these medicines to treat many different illnesses, including asthma, fever, diarrhea, and toothache.

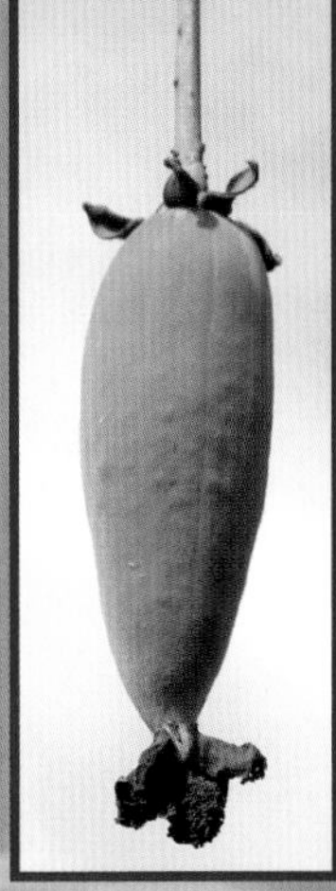

Above: Baobab fruit hanging from a tree
Top left: Inside view of baobab fruit

Baobab fruit being prepared in Botswana

## Snakebite Inoculation

An inoculation is a medical treatment that prevents disease. The flu shot that many people get each year is one example of an inoculation. In Africa, people discovered a way to give inoculations for snakebites.

Africa has always been home to various kinds of snakes. Many of these snakes are poisonous. Snakebites can cause serious medical problems and even death. To protect people from the dangers of snakebite, a medicine was made from the heads of poisonous snakes. First, the heads were dried and ground into a powder, along with leaves from certain plants. Liquid was added to turn the powder into a paste. To inoculate a person, the healer made cuts in the skin on various parts of the body, and then rubbed in a small amount of the paste. More paste was rubbed in every few days for about three weeks.

The green mamba is a poisonous African tree snake.

# ARTS AND CRAFTS

Traditionally, people from various African communities used arts and crafts to show culture, customs, and religious beliefs, and to make everyday objects beautiful. Artists used whatever materials were available in the environment, choosing the ones that were most useful for their purpose.

A traditional Zulu basket from South Africa

## Basket Weaving

Basket weaving has a long history in African cultures. This skill was handed down from parents to children. Some baskets were made from grass, while others were made from reeds or leaves from palm trees. Baskets were used as containers to store or carry goods. Some baskets were so tightly woven that they could hold water.

A woman in Botswana uses palm leaves to weave a traditional basket.

Brightly colored modern African baskets

To make baskets, people often used the coil method:

1) The weaver collected the material to be used. (If palm leaves were used, they were torn into strips for weaving.)
2) The material was dyed different colors. Dyes were made from leaves, tree bark, and flowers. The dyed material was hung to dry.
3) The material was wound into tight coils to create the shape of the basket. To hold the coils in place, the weaver tied them together while creating the basket.

Some baskets had handles and a lid, while others were left open at the top. The weaver used color to create patterns with different meanings. For example, in a Zulu basket made of grass, a checkerboard pattern might represent good news, such as a birth or a plentiful harvest.

## Bark Cloth

Cloth made from tree bark was one of the first types of cloth made by ancient Africans. To make bark cloth, people peeled off strips of the inner layer of bark. They softened the bark with water and then beat it with a rock or wooden mallet to make it even softer. Strips of bark could be sewn together to create a large piece of cloth.

Bark cloth often has interesting patterns. To create patterns, people used the bark from different kinds of trees—the bark from each tree was a different color. Sometimes patterns were painted onto bark cloth.

In later times, some cultural groups used fibers taken from bark and wove them into cloth.

**This costume from Zambia is made of bark fibers and was worn for special ceremonies.**

## Kente Cloth

Cloth weaving in Africa dates back to about 3000 BCE. Cloth used for clothing was made from tree bark, grass, or fibers from palm leaves.

Kente cloth is a special kind of cloth made by the Ashanti people of Ghana. A legend says that Ashanti hunters first learned to create this cloth by watching how a spider wove its web in a forest. When they returned home, the men used fibers from the leaves of the raffia palm to create the first kente cloth.

Modern weavers of kente cloth use cotton, silk, or rayon yarn and the weavers work on a loom. The cloth is woven in strips that are sewn together.

Some kente cloth is designed to be used only by chiefs, while others are for special occasions, such as a wedding, birth, or death.

## Pottery

Pots, dishes, and other items made from clay are called pottery. People in Africa discovered how to make pottery around 7000 BCE, and this craft is still popular today.

Dried clay is brittle, but when pots are heated at high temperatures in an oven or kiln, they become much stronger. Making clay pots requires great skill and practical knowledge. The size and style of a pot depends on how it will be used—for cooking, storing cooked food or grains, holding water, or for use in special ceremonies.

Traditionally, pots were usually made by women, though in western and central Africa men sometimes worked as potters. For example, in Nigeria women made pots for household use and men made pots for community ceremonies.

In some parts of Africa, dyes made from plants were used to add color to pots. Sometimes, designs with human or animal figures were added for decoration.

This traditional pot is decorated with a star and two flowers.

Modern pottery on display in Tunisia

## Hair Braiding

In Africa, hair braiding is an art form that dates as far back as 3500 to 4000 BCE. Each region of Africa has its own traditional style. Sometimes, the style of the braiding communicated a message—one style might show that the person is from a particular village, and another style might show that the person holds an important position in his or her village. Some hair braiding styles were reserved for ceremonial occasions such as weddings.

Cornrows, a style still popular today, is one of the oldest braiding techniques. Cornrow patterns can be straight lines (like rows of corn), zigzag lines, or other patterns.

Girls with cornrows

A man from Burkina Faso wears a traditional mask.

## Masks and Statues

Early Africans made masks and statues from stone, wood, and ivory. (Later on, metals such as gold and bronze were used.) These carved works of art often had special meaning and were used in traditional ceremonies.

Carvers learned their craft from a parent or by training with a local carver. Wood was the material used most often and it was carved using an adze—a special cutting tool that had a curved metal blade. A carver might have two or three different adzes, each with a different size or shape. A small knife was sometimes used to add details to the carving.

Masks and statues were often decorated with feathers, horns, or beads. Different communities created their own special style of carvings.

A small doll statue from Cameroon

## Jewelry

In addition to jewelry made from metal, African people made beautiful beaded bracelets and necklaces from materials such as wood, shells, clay, bone, and seeds. The beads might be strung together using animal sinew or fibers from plants. In some cultures, such as the San people of Botswana, family members and relatives would each give a young child a string of beads. These beads were a symbol of the child's connection to the family group.

An ankle bracelet worn by women in the Sahara region

Traditional jewelry of the Mursi people of Cameroon

Beads worn by Hamer women of Ethiopia

A woman from the Turkana people of Kenya proudly displays her jewelry.

# COMMUNICATION

African peoples developed many interesting ways to communicate messages. They had different techniques for communicating to people over a distance and within a village. Sometimes objects were used as symbols to send a message to a person or group.

The talking drum is hit with a wooden beater.

## Talking Drums

Talking drums were made from wood alone or with animal skin stretched over wood. These drums were used by communities all over Africa to send messages. Each rhythm that a drummer played had a different meaning. For example, one rhythm sent the message that a king had died, and another rhythm warned members of a community that enemies might attack.

Talking drums were made in different sizes. Larger drums made a louder sound, so they were used to send messages to distant places. Smaller drums were easy to carry and were used by messengers as they traveled around a community to deliver a message to the people who lived there.

## Metal Gong

Early Africans made iron gongs in a variety of shapes and sizes. Gongs shaped like a cone were most common. The gongs were beaten with sticks or carved bamboo rods to communicate messages. In countries such as Nigeria, there were special gongs played only by women to announce the death of a woman in the community.

Cone-shaped gongs from Benin

## Woodblocks

Woodblocks were used as a musical instrument as well as to communicate messages. The wooden blocks were hollowed out inside to make a louder sound when they were hit with a wooden stick. Woodblocks might be used to announce a community project or to send a message that people should not harvest a certain type of tree, especially trees used for medicine, so that it would not become too scarce.

A woodblock from Sudan

## Animal Horns

Horns of wild and domesticated animals, such as antelopes, goats, and cows, were used to communicate messages. The horns were hollowed out and a person blew into one end of the horn to create a sound, similar to the way a musician blows into a trumpet.

To send messages over a long distance, the horn blower might climb to the top of a house, a tree, or a hill.

Animal horns were often used in times of war. Horns were blown to inform people to be alert for an attack or to gather people together in preparation for a battle. The horns could also be blown to call people together to settle a quarrel or to announce that a quarrel had been settled.

In the 2010 FIFA World Cup soccer games in South Africa, fans showed their support by blowing plastic horns called vuvuzelas. Traditional vuvuzelas were made from the horns of the kudu (a type of antelope) and were used to call people to attend community meetings.

**Right: The kudu has magnificent curved horns. Below left: A Maasai warrior plays a traditional horn. Below right: This modern plastic vuvuzela is decorated with beads.**

## Kola Nuts

Kola nuts were harvested from trees and presented to a visitor as a sign of peace, friendship, or hospitality. The fresh nuts were chewed as part of a greeting ceremony. This custom is still followed today, particularly in Nigeria.

**Kola nuts are also used to make modern cola drinks.**

## Palm Fronds

The leader of a village or group might use palm fronds (leaves) to communicate important public or private messages. For example, a village elder might send a palm frond to someone who was accused of doing something wrong. This carried the message that the person should not take part in community activities until he or she was proven innocent. When a group was traveling, religious leaders dropped palm fronds on the ground to let people know when they were close to a place of worship.

## Rock Paintings

African peoples created rock paintings showing humans and animals. These paintings communicated a group's religious and cultural beliefs. Ancient rock paintings have been discovered all across the African continent, including in countries such as Algeria, Egypt, Libya, Namibia, Niger, Zimbabwe, Botswana, and Somalia.

Rock art in Africa is believed to have deep religious significance. In southern Africa the paintings show traditional healers or shamans performing ceremonies to heal the sick. Some rock art has scenes showing rain-making rituals and symbols that people believed would attract animals for the hunt. Many African rock art sites have been declared UNESCO World Heritage Sites.

**Left and below: Two examples of prehistoric rock art from South Africa show hunting scenes.**

The famous Rosetta Stone

Hieroglyphics uses pictures and symbols.

## Egyptian Hieroglyphics

Ancient Egyptians developed different forms of writing to record information. The most famous form of ancient Egyptian writing is called hieroglyphics.

Hieroglyphics does not use an alphabet. Instead, it uses pictures and symbols (called hieroglyphs) to represent objects, ideas, actions, and sounds. Some words could be written using one hieroglyph. Other words were written using more than one hieroglyph.

Ancient Egyptians used hieroglyphics mostly for writing on the walls of temples and tombs, such as the pyramids. They had a different form of writing for everyday use. Around 400 CE, Egyptians stopped using hieroglyphics. Soon there was no one left who knew how to read this written language.

In 1799 CE, a French soldier in Egypt discovered a slab of stone that had writing carved in it. The writing was in Greek, hieroglyphics, and another form of Egyptian writing. This important discovery was called the Rosetta Stone.

Experts realized that the stone had one text written three times—once in each of the three forms of writing. A language expert named Jean-Francois Champollion spent two years studying the writing on the stone, and was finally able to understand the hieroglyphics. Thanks to his work, experts were able to translate hieroglyphics found in ancient Egyptian buildings and understand much more about how ancient Egyptians lived.

## Town Crier

A town crier traveled around a community, announcing messages in a loud voice. African chiefs used town criers to communicate information to people. The town crier might call out important announcements about local laws or information about market days or missing persons.

Town criers are still active in some places in Africa. They beat a gong to attract people's attention and then read out a message from the king or chief.

# FOOD

Traditional African communities developed unique foods and used different ways to preserve food so it would last longer. Some African foods have become popular around the world.

Today, Africans still sometimes dry meat to preserve it.

## Meat Preservation

After hunters had killed an animal, they had to preserve the meat so it would not begin to rot. Drying meat in the sun was one way to preserve it. Hunters cut the meat into small strips, hung them over sticks or lines, and left them in the sun to dry. People preferred this method because it helped the meat keep its natural flavor.

Drying meat in the sun took time. When hunters were in a hurry to move to another place, they used the faster method of smoking meat to preserve it. The meat was placed over smoke from a fire. Once the meat was dry, it was stored in special baskets or in clay pots.

Cassava for sale in a market in Morocco

## Fermentation

Fermentation is a chemical change in food that helps prevent it from spoiling. Some foods become more nutritious or easier to digest once they have been fermented. Certain foods ferment on their own, and sometimes people add things to a food to make it ferment. Cheese and yogurt are examples of foods popular today that are made from fermented milk.

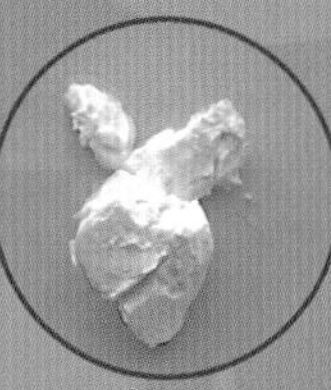

Yam

Traditional African peoples fermented milk, yams, cassava, and other foods. The process of fermenting foods required skill and took some time to learn. This skill was passed on from one generation to the next.

## Warankasi

The Fulani people of Nigeria developed a method for fermenting milk and using it to make a soft cheese called warankasi. This cheese provided people with a good source of protein when little meat or fish was available.

Warankasi and other soft white cheeses are popular in many parts of Africa.

To make warankasi, juice squeezed from the leaves of a particular plant is mixed with milk and heated to make the milk ferment. Soon soft lumps called curds form. These are removed and placed in a basket. Once some of the liquid has drained out of the curds and they are the right consistency, the warankasi is ready.

The San people filled ostrich eggs with water, plugged the hole with grass, and then buried the egg to keep the water cool.

## Ugali

Ugali is a traditional food that is especially popular in southern and eastern areas of Africa. (It is sometimes called *sadza*, *tshimanga*, *posha*, or *parechi*.)

Ugali is often made from corn meal, although other types of grain may be used. The corn meal is slowly added to a pot of boiling water, which is stirred constantly. When the mixture becomes thicker than mashed potatoes, it is ready. Ugali is dipped into stew or, like fufu (to the right), used to scoop up food.

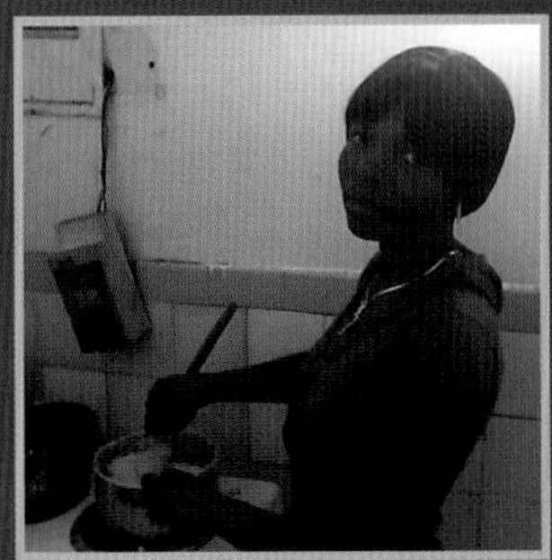

**A Maasai woman sterilizes a calabash gourd with a stick that is glowing hot at one end. Then she will insert a narrow hollow piece into the opening and use the gourd to feed her child.**

## Fufu

Fufu is a traditional food enjoyed by people in the western and central areas of Africa. Today, some people still use a traditional method to make it. Cassava or yams are boiled and pounded together, sometimes with other foods such as corn. This makes a very thick paste, similar to a dough, that can be formed into a large circular shape. People tear off a small piece of fufu and use it to scoop up soup or stew.

**A woman from Liberia pounds cassava to make fufu.**

**Injera may be served with other foods on top.**

## Injera

Injera is a spongy bread that was first made in Ethiopia. Traditionally, people used flour made from teff (a cereal grain) to make injera. Water and salt were mixed with the teff flour to create a dough. The dough was then put aside for three days before it was placed on a large clay plate called a *mogogo* and baked over a fire.

*For information on some foods that grow in Africa, see pages 14–15.*

# MUSICAL INSTRUMENTS

Music is an important part of African cultures, and various communities developed different styles of music and different musical instruments. In traditional African cultures, music was a form of entertainment and was also part of important ceremonies. People might clap, dance, and sing along as music was played on various instruments.

Many of these instruments are still played today, and African music has influenced music around the world.

## Kora

Also called the African harp, the kora has been popular in West African countries, such as Guinea, The Gambia, Sierra Leone, Senegal, Mali, and Burkina Faso. A kora usually has 21 strings, but some have as many as 25.

The bottom part of a kora is made from a large gourd cut in half and covered with animal skin. Traditional koras have strings made of animal sinew, which are attached to sticks that run through the gourd. Musicians use the thumb and index fingers of both hands to play the kora.

A traditional kora from Mali

## Mbira

The mbira is sometimes called a thumb piano, but it is also known by several different names across Africa. It can have as few as 7 or as many as 22 to 28 metal keys, which are played with both thumbs and the right index finger. Sometimes the mbira is placed inside a calabash gourd, which helps to make the sound louder. Small objects such as beads or shells are often attached to the wooden base of the mbira. These create a buzzing or rattling sound, which adds to the music.

## Nyatiti

The nyatiti is a stringed instrument that is often close to 1 meter (3 feet) long. It is popular with the Luo people, who live mostly in Kenya. To play a nyatiti, the musician sits on a low stool and holds the instrument close to the chest. Often, the nyatiti is played together with the oporo, an instrument made from an antelope horn with a gourd attached at the end.

A young man from Kenya with his nyatiti

A kosika from Burkina Faso

## Kosika

The kosika is a percussion instrument that is popular in Ghana, Mali, and Cameroon. It is made from two small gourds filled with seeds. The two gourds are tied together with a short piece of string.

To play a kosika, the player holds one gourd in one hand and shakes it like a rattle. While shaking the one gourd, the player makes the gourd at the other end of the string swing around in a circle so that it hits the gourd held in the hand. This makes a "clack" sound that adds to the rhythm.

In Ghana, the kosika is mainly a children's toy. In Mali, only women and children play the kosika. Villagers in Cameroon play their kosikas whenever their chief enters the room.

## Rattles

There are many different types of rattles used among African communities. Some rattles are made from gourds filled with seeds. The gourds are then covered with animal skin. Traditionally, men and women wore the rattles when dancing.

The Zulu people of South Africa make beautiful ankle rattles from small gourds filled with seeds or sand. People wear these around their ankles when dancing, or sometimes they just shake the rattles with their hands.

Zulu ankle rattles

Various African rattles

## Marimba

Experts believe that the marimba (often called a xylophone) was invented in what is now the country of Mali, about 700 years ago. A marimba is made from wooden planks, all different sizes, which are usually set into a frame. The shorter planks make high notes and the longer planks make low notes. To play the marimba, the wooden planks are hit with a wooden mallet.

There are different kinds of marimbas. Some have short legs and the musician sits while playing. A pit xylophone sits over a hole in the ground. The echo from the hole makes the sound louder.

From Africa, the marimba spread around the world and it is still a popular instrument today.

*Drums are an important instrument in African music and they were also used for communication.* *For more information on drums, see page 28.*

# GAMES AND SPORTS

The peoples of Africa developed many different games and sports. Some were forms of entertainment and recreation. Others helped people to develop skills that were necessary for survival.

## Bao

Bao is one example of a family of games called mancala games. In these games, players move their game pieces on a board and try to capture their opponent's playing pieces. In this way, mancala games are similar to chess and checkers. Some experts believe that mancala games were first developed in Ethiopia around the 6th or 7th century CE.

Bao is a traditional African game played by two people. The game board is made of wood, with two or four rows of holes carved into it. Pebbles, stones, or seeds are used as playing pieces. The object of the game is to capture the most playing pieces.

A traditional bao game

A modern mancala game

## Nhodo

Nhodo is a traditional African game that is popular with young girls. It is similar to the game we know as jacks.

To play nhodo, players sit around a small hole in the ground. For playing pieces, they use pebbles or sometimes seeds. One larger pebble is chosen as the one that is not allowed to hit the ground. Using just one hand, a player throws the large pebble in the air and catches it. While this pebble is in the air, the player adds or removes other pebbles to or from the hole. This is tricky because the player must throw and catch the large pebble, and move the smaller pebbles, using just one hand. The smaller pebbles are first moved one at a time, then two at a time, and so on. If the player lets the large pebble fall to the ground, the next person takes a turn.

This game helps children learn to count, and it also teaches them to watch carefully and make quick and accurate hand movements.

These game pieces are used to play jacks, which is similar to nhodo.

## Spear and Rungu Throwing

In traditional societies in the eastern and southern parts of Africa, men held contests to see who could throw a spear or a club (called a *rungu*) the longest distance. These contests helped to train young warriors in strength and accuracy. The Maasai and Turkana peoples of Kenya used spears that were 2 to 3 meters (6 to 10 feet) long.

A Maasai warrior throws a spear. He uses his walking stick to help him aim.

Left and right: Zulu dancers perform traditional dances.

## Competitive Dancing

Throughout history, dancing has been an important part of life for African peoples. They danced during religious ceremonies and to mark important occasions, such as a birth, marriage, or death. There were special dancing styles for each kind of event, and various communities developed their own dancing styles.

Dance competitions are popular today, especially in African schools. Dance helps to preserve the cultures of African peoples, and it also helps the dancers stay physically fit.

## Stick Fighting

Stick fighting was a form of martial arts popular with communities in Angola, Mozambique, South Africa, Swaziland, Zimbabwe, Ethiopia, Nigeria, Kenya, and Tanzania. The sticks were about as long as a walking stick or sometimes longer. This sport helped men to develop the courage, skills, and endurance they would need as warriors and hunters.

Mursi warriors from Ethiopia practice their stick fighting skills.

## Wrestling

Wrestling was a popular sport in communities in western, eastern, and southern Africa. For young men, wrestling was an important part of the ceremonies that marked the change from childhood to adulthood.

Young boys often wrestled for fun, while warriors wrestled to stay in good shape for combat. In Cameroon, wrestling was used as a way of settling arguments. In some communities, women also wrestled. In western and northern Africa, women would wrestle each year after the harvest.

Wrestling is still popular today in some African cultures, and the best wrestlers become famous.

Spectators cheer at a traditional wresting competition in Kenya.

# AFRICA TODAY

Today, Africa is an interesting mix of old and new. In large modern cities, many aspects of life are similar to life in a large North American city. But there are still places in Africa where the traditions of the past are an important part of daily life.

This luxurious hotel in Khartoum, Sudan, attracts many business travelers.

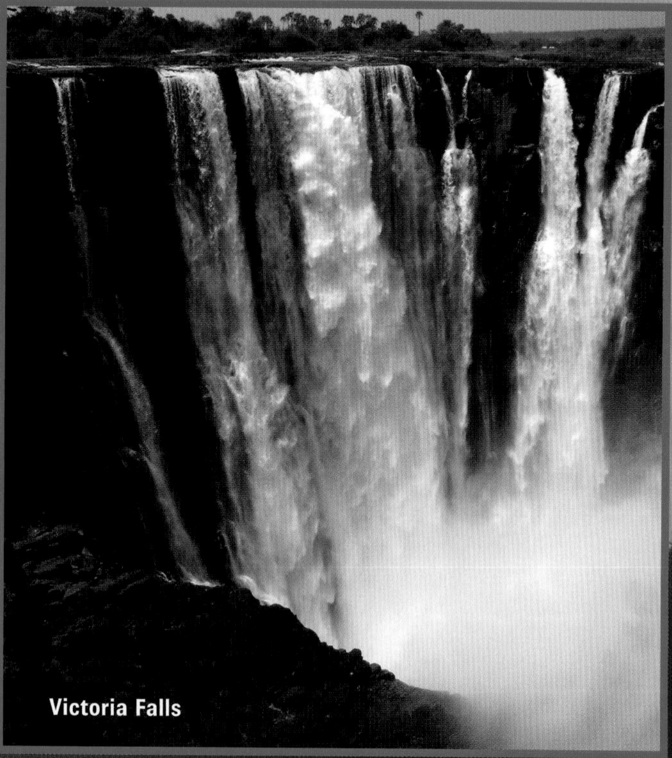

Victoria Falls

## Tourism

Africa is a popular destination for tourists. In Tanzania, visitors can go on a safari to view wildlife in Serengeti National Park or they can climb Mount Kilimanjaro, Africa's tallest mountain.

In Ghana, tourists can learn about the horrors of slavery by visiting the "slave castles" where Africans were imprisoned before they were shipped overseas to be sold as slaves.

Victoria Falls, located on the border between Zambia and Zimbabwe, is one of the most famous waterfalls in the world.

From the pyramids of Egypt in the north to the beautiful beaches of South Africa, the African continent offers many great experiences for tourists.

## The Nobel Peace Prize

The Nobel Peace Prize is awarded to a person or organization that promotes peace in the world. This prize is considered a very great honor, and it has been awarded to Africans eight times. Recent winners of this prize include Mohamed ElBaradei (Egypt), Wangari Maathai (Kenya), Kofi Annan (Ghana), and Nelson Mandela (South Africa).

A former Secretary-General of the United Nations, Kofi Annan won the Nobel Peace Prize in 2001.

In 2004, Wangari Maathai became the first African woman to win the Nobel Peace Prize.

A teen dances to hip hop music.

## African Music and Dance

The rhythms, melodies, and instruments of traditional African music have influenced music all over the world. When African musicians moved to places outside Africa, they took their musical traditions with them. Many types music popular today have been influenced by the sounds of African music. For example:

| REGION | TYPE OF MUSIC |
|---|---|
| Brazil | Samba |
| The Caribbean | Reggae, calypso |
| North America | Gospel, blues, jazz, rock, hip hop |

African forms of dance have also had an influence around the world. The samba from Brazil, the merengue from Venezuela, as well as the rumba and mambo from Cuba, are all dances that have links to the traditions of Africa.

## Information Technology

Information technology (storing and sending information with computers) is an industry that is growing quickly in Africa.

New advances in cell phone technology make it possible for Africans in rural areas to have access to telephone service, as well services such as telephone banking.

African countries are working closely with nations from outside Africa to help the information technology industry grow even stronger.

The people of Africa recognize the importance of preserving wildlife.

## Environment

Like many countries around the world, African countries are concerned about preserving their unique natural environments and the animals and plants that live in these environments. Governments and non-profit organizations in many African countries have developed programs to help preserve the environment and raise awareness of environmental issues. There are also programs that allow young people to get involved with this important cause, such as the Africa Environment Outlook for Youth.

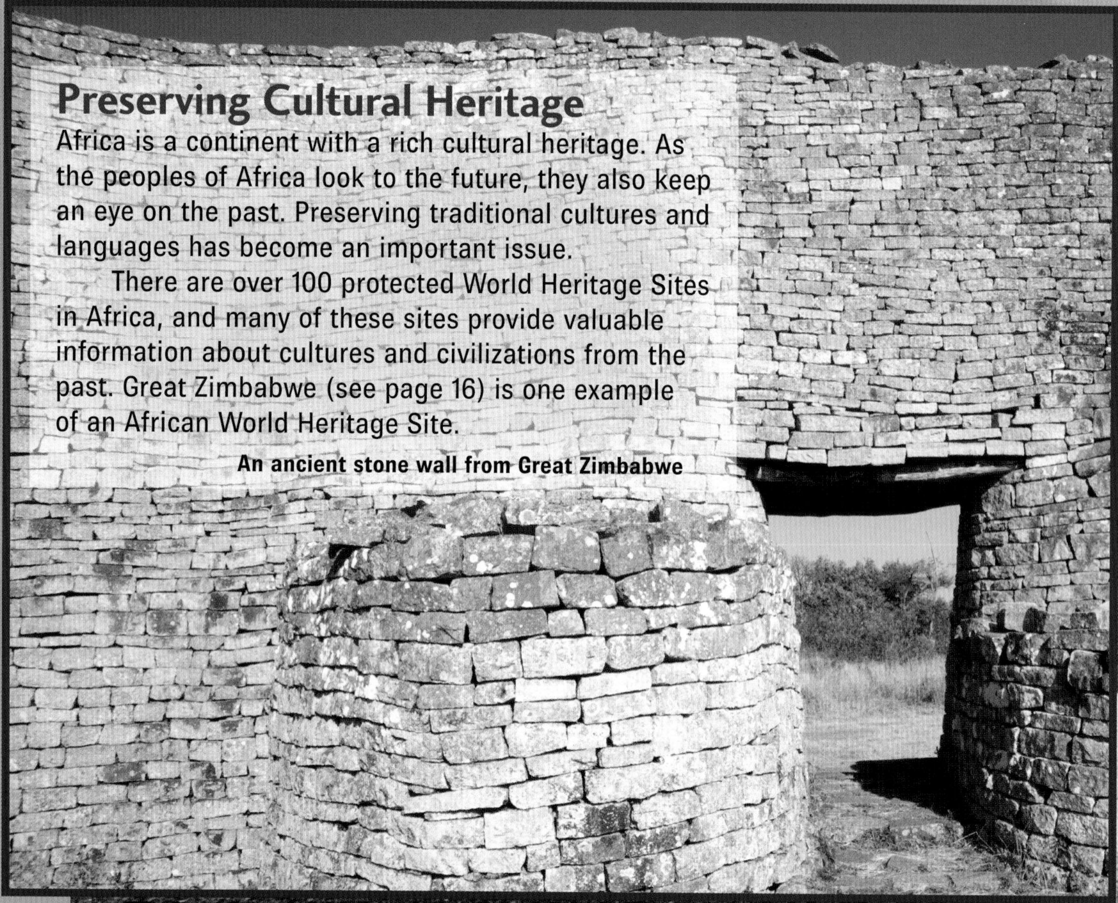

## Preserving Cultural Heritage

Africa is a continent with a rich cultural heritage. As the peoples of Africa look to the future, they also keep an eye on the past. Preserving traditional cultures and languages has become an important issue.

There are over 100 protected World Heritage Sites in Africa, and many of these sites provide valuable information about cultures and civilizations from the past. Great Zimbabwe (see page 16) is one example of an African World Heritage Site.

**An ancient stone wall from Great Zimbabwe**

## Mining and Drilling

Mining for minerals is one of the most important industries in Africa. Almost half of the diamonds produced in the world come from Africa, with Botswana producing the most diamonds. Other important minerals mined in Africa include platinum and gold (mainly from South Africa), uranium (mainly from Namibia and Niger), and copper (mainly from the Democratic Republic of the Congo and Zambia).

Drilling for oil and natural gas is another important industry. Four African countries (Nigeria, Algeria, Angola, and Libya) are among the top 20 oil producers in the world.

**An oil rig under construction off the coast of Namibia**

**An oil rig off the coast of Egypt**

## Sports

Africa has produced many fine athletes and sports teams. Zimbabwean swimmer Kirsty Coventry has set world records and was one of the top medal winners in the 2008 Olympics.

African athletes have been particularly strong in track and field events. In the 2008 Olympics, 11 gold medals for track and field events went to athletes from African countries—six medals for Kenya, four for Ethiopia, and one for Cameroon.

South Africa proudly hosted the 2010 FIFA World Cup, an international soccer competition. Teams from Algeria, Cameroon, Ghana, Ivory Coast, Nigeria, and South Africa took part in the competition, with Ghana advancing to the quarter-finals.

**Ethiopian long-distance runner Meseret Defar has won many medals, including a gold medal at the 2004 Olympics.**

**The Moses Mabhida Stadium in Durban, South Africa, hosted games for the 2010 FIFA World Cup soccer competition.**

## From the Past to the Future

Africa has overcome many challenges of the past, including the slave trade and control by European nations. The peoples of Africa have shown strength and dignity in overcoming these challenges. For example, for many years black South Africans suffered discrimination and cruel treatment from their government. This policy was known as Apartheid. Apartheid ended with the election of South Africa's first black president, Nelson Mandela. The new government did not take revenge on the people responsible for Apartheid. Instead of sending these people to prison, a Truth and Reconciliation Commission was established. People who had been guilty of injustices to the black population were allowed to apologize for their actions and were forgiven.

Today, Africans continue to face many challenges—wars, food shortages, poverty, and health issues such as AIDS. But as the innovations in this book have shown, the people of Africa have a long history of coming up with creative solutions to challenges. This history, along with the courage and determination displayed by people all over Africa, suggest that there is every reason to be optimistic about the future of this great continent.

**For many young people in Africa, the future looks bright.**

# A BRIEF TIMELINE OF AFRICA

## Before 1500 CE

In several different regions of Africa, great empires with prosperous cities appear. These empires include ancient civilizations in Egypt, Nubia (now called Sudan), and Zimbabwe (see "Great Zimbabwe" on page 16.)

**The Great Sphinx of Giza is one of many architectural masterpieces created by the ancient Egyptians.**

## 1500–1800 CE

The slave trade begins. Millions of Africans are forced from their homes and sold as slaves in countries such as Jamaica, Cuba, Barbados, Haiti, Brazil, Portugal, England, and Holland, as well as in areas of North America that eventually became part of the United States. Most slaves are transported on English ships.

**These African men, women, and children were captured to be sold as slaves.**

## 1800–1956 CE

In the early 1800s, European countries, as well as the United States, end the slave trade. Countries such as England, France, and Germany divide most of Africa into colonies, which they control. Schools, railways, and highways are built, but most of the wealth from African gold, copper, and diamonds goes to Europe and the Americas.

**The Uganda Railway was built by the British government. Construction began in 1896 CE.**

## 1956–1990 CE

During this period, over 50 African countries win the right to govern themselves. In the 1980s, the AIDS epidemic begins and affects Africa more than other continents. Sadly, this epidemic reverses some of the gains made in African countries after they won independence.

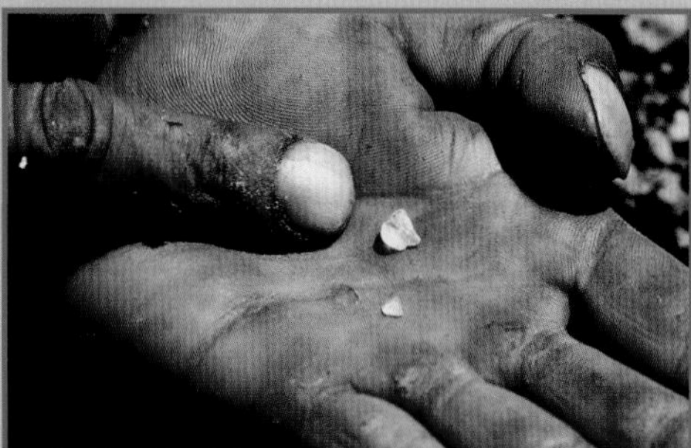

**Uncut diamonds from an African mine**

## 1990–Present

In the country of South Africa, the 1990s brings the end of a policy known as Apartheid. Under this policy, a small minority of white South Africans ruled harshly over non-white citizens, who made up about 90 percent of the country's population. Nelson Mandela is elected as the first black president of South Africa in 1994.

**Nelson Mandela was jailed for fighting against Apartheid. He is shown here after his release from jail in 1990.**

# Further Reading


Bingham, J. *African Art and Culture.* London: Heinemann, 2003.

Hansen, J. *African Princess: The Amazing Lives of Africa's Royal Women.* New York: Hyperion Books, 2005.

Ibazebo, S. *Africa: Exploring History.* London: Belitha Press, 2003.

Porter, M. *An Illustrated Atlas of Africa (Continents in Close-up series).* London: The Evans Publishing Group, 2008.

Richardson, H. *Life in Ancient Africa (Peoples of the Ancient World series).* New York: Crabtree, 2005.

Sherrow, V. *Ancient Africa: Archaeology Unlocks the Secrets of Africa's Past.* Washington, DC: National Geographic Society, 2007.


## Selected Sources


Connah, G. *Forgotten Africa: An Introduction to Its Archaeology.* London and New York: Routledge, 2004.

Crowther, B. N. *Sport in Ancient Times.* Westport, CT: Praeger Publications, 2007.

Ehret, C. *The Civilizations of Africa: A History to 1800.* Charlottesville, VA: University Press of Virginia, 2002.

Gates, H. L. *Wonders of the African World.* New York: Alfred A. Knopf, 1999.

Iwu, M. M. *Handbook of African Medicinal Plants.* Ann Arbor, MI: CRC Press, 1993.

Mitchell, P. *African Connections: Archaeological Perspectives on Africa and the Wider World.* Walnut Creek, CA: Alta Mira Press, 2005.

Onwuejeogwu, M. A., Okpu, B., & Ebighgbo, C. *African Civilizations: Origin, Growth and Development.* Lagos, Nigeria: UTO Publications, 2000.

Vogel, J. O. (Ed.). *Ancient African Metallurgy: The Socio-Cultural Context.* Walnut Creek, CA: Alta Mira Press, 2000.

# Credits

**Front cover right, 16 left top, 16 left bottom,** Dariusz Wiejaczka; **3, 17 left bottom,** Anke Van Wyk; **5 right top, back cover background, 6-7 top, 6 background left,** Dmitryp; **5 right bottom,** Dsukhov; **5 left top, 41 middle left, 41 background,** Instinia Photography; **5 left middle,** Nigel Monckton; **5 left bottom, 36 second,** Kenneth Sponsler; **7 middle,** Ppmaker2007; **7 bottom,** Darren Patterson; **8-9 top,** Paul Hampton; **9 right top,** Sam Downes; **9 right middle,** Lucian Coman; **10, 11, 37 bottom background,** António Jorge Da Silva Nunes; **13 left top,** Marius Scarlat; **14 top background,** Jujuba74; **14 bottom,** Galyna Andrushko; **15 background,** Szefei; **15 top left,** Zakaria Adli Idrus; **15 right,** Brian Longmore; **16 background,** Vladimir Melnik; **17 top,** Andre Klaassen; **17 right bottom, back cover second,** Bernardo Ertl; **18-19 background,** Tiziano Casalta; **18 right top,** Fokinol; **21 right, 27 bottom right,** Uros Ravbar; **22 middle,** Zheng Dong; **22 bottom,** Grondin Franck Olivier; **23 top second,** Nina Ricci Fedotova; **23 top third,** Cubrazol; **23 bottom,** Arievdwolde; **23 background,** Kira Kaplinski; **24 background,** Nico Smit; **26 middle right,** Exinocactus; **26 background,** Wessel Cirkel; **27 middle right, 29 top,** Neal Cooper; **29 left,** Anna Omelchenko; **30 top,** Jamie Watson; **30 middle,** Anthony Baggett; **30 background,** John Casey; **31 bottom, back cover fifth,** Swisshippo; **32 right top,** Roger De Montfort; **32 right middle,** Findlay Rankin; **32 left top,** Dennis Owusu-ansah; **36 third,** Scott Rothstein; **38 top left,** Daniel Loncarevic; **38, top right,** Riana444; **38 background,** Javarman; **39 top,** Erwin Purnomo Sidi; **39 middle,** Ron Chapple Studios; **39 bottom left,** Eszawa; **39 bottom right,** Pixworld; **39 background,** Jiří Kasal; **40 top,** David Snyder; **40 bottom,** Argironeta; **40 background,** Martesia Bezuidenhout; **41 top,** Sportgraphic; **41 middle right,** Grosremy; **41 bottom,** Hongqi Zhang; **42 first,** Sculpies; **42 fourth,** Fabrizio Argonauta; **42 background, 43,** Nico Smit; **47 background,** Ami Levin. All ©Dreamstime.com. **Front cover left, 25 bottom, 33 left middle second,** Peeter Viisimaa; **8 middle, 12 middle, 17 middle, back cover first, 33 left bottom, 36 first, 36 fourth,** Britta Kasholm-Tengve; **12 top,** Johan Swanepoel; **12 bottom,** Joost van Sluijters; **15 middle left,** Guenter Guni; **15 bottom left,** Michau van Gass; **18 left bottom, 19 bottom,** Diane Miller; **24 top right,** Joe McDaniel; **24 bottom right,** Grace Donald; **26 top right,** Diane Peacock; **26 bottom right,** Hans Martens; **27 middle,** Warwick Lister-Kaye; **27 top left,** Alida Vanni; **27 bottom left, back cover third,** Diane White Rosier; **29 right, 35 top fourth top,** Cliff Parnell; **30 bottom,** Anton Ferreira; **33 right top,** MShep2; **33 right bottom, back cover fourth,** narvikk; **34 middle,** Emily Ryan; **35 top first,** Raido Väljamaa; **35 top second,** cale Anderson; **35 top fourth bottom,** sebastian-k; **35 bottom first,** Don Bayley; **35 bottom second,** HultonArchive; **37 top left, 37 top right,** Steven Allan; **40 bottom inset,** Mlenny. All ©iStockphoto, Inc. **6 left inset, 47 left,** ©Arnold Mayaka. **8 bottom,** Remi Benali/The Image Bank/Getty Images. **9 bottom,** courtesy Melissa Heckler. **13 right top, 20 left bottom, 21 all left,** Museum of Anthropology, University of Missouri. **13 left bottom,** ©Anthony Bannister; Gallo Images/CORBIS; **16 right,** ©Colin Hoskins; Cordaiy Photo Library Ltd./CORBIS; **22 top,** ©STR/Reuters/Corbis; **24 left,** ©Gallo Images/CORBIS; **25 top,** ©David Reed/CORBIS; **37 bottom,** ©DAI KUROKAWA/epa/Corbis. **13 right bottom, 18 right middle, 23 top first,** ©Richard B. Lee. **14 top,** ©DE AGOSTINI EDITORE PICTURE LIBRARY/Dorling Kindersley; **28 top,** ©Dorling Kindersley; **28 middle,** Philip Dowell ©Dorling Kindersley; **28 bottom,** ©Dorling Kindersley, courtesy of the Powell-Cotton Museum, Kent. **18 left top,** AP.0.0.952, collection RMCA Tervuren; photo Michel, 1898. **18 right bottom,** The Art Archive/Rijksmuseum voor Volkenkunde Leiden (Leyden)/Gianni Dagli Orti; **20 right,** The Art Archive/British Library; **27 top right,** The Art Archive/Antenna Gallery Dakar Senegal/Gianni Dagli Orti; **31 top,** The Art Archive/British Museum/Alfredo Dagli Orti. **20 left top,** Rosser1954: http://en.wikipedia.org/w/index.php?title=Manillas&oldid=395321360; **20 left middle,** Rosser1954: http://en.wikipedia.org/w/index.php?title=Katanga_Cross&oldid=389681963; **32 left bottom,** Omernos: http://en.wikipedia.org/w/index.php?title= Strained_yoghurt&oldid=395545316. **32 right bottom, 34 bottom, 37 middle,** ©Ariadne Van Zandbergen. **33 left top first, second, left middle first,** ©Dede and Sandra Kamani. **34 top,** ©Canadian Museum of Civilization, no. 2000.139.9, IMG2008-0231-0001-Dm. **35 top third,** ©2010 Jupiterimages Corporation. **38 bottom left,** AFOLABI SOTUNDE/Reuters/Landov; **38 bottom right,** YVES HERMAN/Reuters/Landov; **42 fifth,** JUDA NGWENYA/Reuters/Landov. **42 second,** *The Graphic*, London: June 7, 1884, p. 548, Library of Congress, LC-DIG-ppmsca-15836; **42 third,** Phelps Publishing Co., Library of Congress, LC-USZ62-65505. **47 right,** ©Lucah Rosenberg-Lee.

# Index

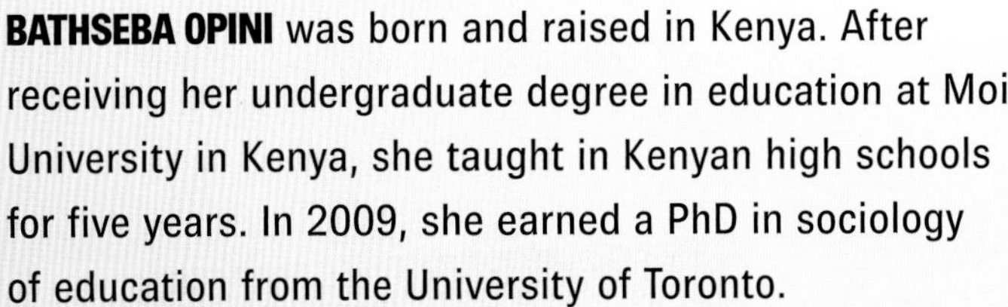

**BATHSEBA OPINI** was born and raised in Kenya. After receiving her undergraduate degree in education at Moi University in Kenya, she taught in Kenyan high schools for five years. In 2009, she earned a PhD in sociology of education from the University of Toronto.

Bathseba is the author of the forthcoming book *The Experiences of Women Students with Disabilities in Kenyan University Education*, as well as a number of journal articles and book chapters. In addition to her work with various community organizations focusing on issues of disability, she has taught at Ryerson University and George Brown College. Currently, she is an instructor in the Teacher Education and African Studies programs at the University of Toronto. Bathseba's areas of interest for teaching and research include African indigenous cultural knowledge, international and comparative education (with a focus on Sub-Saharan Africa), HIV/AIDS, anti-racist education, and social inequalities.

**RICHARD B. LEE** is a university professor emeritus in anthropology at the University of Toronto. While still a student, he made his first trip to Africa and spent a year living with the San people of Botswana. In the 1960s, as a young professor at Harvard, Richard returned to Africa to spend two years with the San. In the 1970s and 1980s he was very involved with the anti-Apartheid movement in Namibia and South Africa. He currently travels to Africa each year to supervise training programs for local and foreign students in Namibia in the fight against HIV/AIDS. A Fellow of the Royal Society of Canada, Richard has written or edited seven books and many articles on Africa, anthropology, and hunters and gatherers.

# Also in Annick's acclaimed We Thought of It series:

- ★ "The Year's Best" List, *Resource Links*
- ★ Children's Non-Fiction Top 10 List, Ontario Library Association
- ★ Best Books for Kids & Teens 2008, starred selection, Canadian Children's Book Centre
- ★ 2008 Skipping Stones Honor Award
- ★ 2009 Silver Birch Award nomination

"... chock-a-block full of interesting information and pictures."
—*CM Magazine*

"[An] informative and easy to read book ... attractive and useful."
—*Children's Book News*

- ★ Best Books for Kids & Teens 2009, Canadian Children's Book Centre
- ★ "The Year's Best" List, *Resource Links*
- ★ 2010/2011 Red Cedar Book Award nomination

"... deserves a permanent spot on any reader's bookshelf..."
—*ForeWord Reviews*

"A real eye-opener to enlighten children and adults alike..."
—*Resource Links*

- ★ Best Bets List, Ontario Library Association
- ★ 2010 Best Books, Canadian Children's Book Centre

"A well-focused introduction to the history of technological innovation in China."
—*Booklist Online*

"... an informative and entertaining read."
—*ForeWord Reviews*

**Go to www.annickpress.com to view book trailers for these and other exciting titles.**